Micro gestures for Macro Success

Minor adjustments for Prosperity in Business and Finance"

Williams L.Batts

Copyright © [2024] [Williams L.Batts]

Table of Contents

Table of Contents

Introduction

In the bustling metropolis of corporate dynamism, where boardrooms echoed with the clangour of ambitious deals and the stock market danced to the rhythm of financial intricacies, there existed a subtle force that often went unnoticed—the essence of micro gestures in business and finance.

Meet Olivia Stirling, a seasoned executive with a keen eye for the finer details that set the stage for success. Olivia had learned over the years that beneath the surface of high-stakes negotiations and complex financial manoeuvres, the language of micro-gestures held the key to unlocking unparalleled prosperity. It was a language spoken in the flicker of an eyelid, the firmness of a handshake, and the sincerity of a smile.

As Olivia navigated through the intricate world of mergers and acquisitions, she became attuned to the power of non-verbal communication. In meetings where millions hung in the balance, it was the subtle nod of agreement or the slight furrow of the brow that conveyed more than words ever could. Micro-gestures became her secret weapon, allowing her to build bridges and establish trust in the competitive realm of business.

One day, as Olivia prepared for a crucial negotiation with a potential partner, she found herself immersed in the nuances of micro-gestures. She understood that the first impression was not merely about the exchange of business cards but was shaped by the confident posture and genuine interest displayed through micro gestures. A firm handshake communicated strength and reliability, while maintaining eye contact conveyed sincerity and authenticity.

In the midst of negotiations, Olivia noticed a micro-gesture from the other party—a subtle raise of the eyebrows indicating surprise at a proposal. This small cue allowed Olivia to adjust her approach, tailoring her pitch to address the concerns subtly expressed. The result was a successful collaboration that not only solidified the deal but also laid the foundation for a lasting business relationship.

As Olivia extended her exploration of micro-gestures into the realm of leadership, she discovered the profound impact these subtle cues had on team dynamics. A supportive pat on the back, a nod of acknowledgment, or even a well-timed pause during a conversation—these micro-gestures fostered a culture of collaboration and trust within her team. The essence of leadership, it seemed, lay not only in grand gestures but in the accumulation of small, meaningful actions.

The financial landscape, too, bore witness to the transformative power of micro-gestures. Olivia, guided by the principles of wise financial micro-gestures, implemented small changes in her personal financial habits. Automated savings, conscious spending decisions, and strategic investments became her daily rituals. Over time, these seemingly minor actions accumulated into a substantial financial portfolio, showcasing the macro impact of micro gestures in wealth accumulation.

As Olivia reflected on her journey, she realised that the essence of micro gestures in business and finance was not just about communication or leadership—it was a philosophy that permeated every aspect of success. It was a recognition that in the grand tapestry of professional life, the smallest threads of intention and awareness could weave the most intricate patterns of prosperity.

In the end, Olivia Stirling became not just a business leader but a maestro of micro-gestures, conducting the symphony of success in a world that often overlooked the beauty of subtlety. The essence of micro-gestures had become her legacy, a testament to the transformative power of small changes for prosperity in business and finance.**

Micro Gestures For Macro Success

Minor Adjustments for Prosperity in Business and Finance

Williams L. Batts

Chapter 1

Understanding Micro gestures

In the opening term, "Understanding Micro gestures," readers embark on a journey to unravel the hidden language of subtle cues that shape the intricate tapestry of business success. At its core, the chapter delves into the very definition of micro gestures, those often-overlooked signals that wield remarkable influence in professional interactions.

Defining Micro-gestures: The term begins by establishing a clear and concise definition of micro gesture.

These are the minuscule, non-verbal expressions that subtly convey emotions, intentions, and attitudes. From a raised eyebrow to a fleeting smile, micro-gestures provide a nuanced layer to communication that extends beyond spoken words. Readers are introduced to the idea that mastering this subtle language can be a game-changer in the realm of business dynamics.

Role of Micro gestures in Business Success: As the narrative unfolds, the spotlight turns towards the pivotal role micro gestures play in achieving triumph in the business arena. Understanding that communication extends far beyond verbal discourse, the chapter emphasises how astute recognition and utilisation of micro-gestures can enhance negotiation skills, build trust, and foster meaningful connections.

The exploration of micro-gestures as a tool for deciphering hidden meanings and intentions sets the stage for the overarching theme of the book—how these seemingly minor actions can collectively contribute to macro success. Readers are prompted to reflect on their own experiences, perhaps recalling instances where a subtle nod or a well-timed pause significantly influenced the course of a professional interaction.

In essence, "Understanding Micro gestures" serves as the foundation for the subsequent chapters, laying the groundwork for readers to delve deeper into the intricacies of non-verbal communication and recognize the immense potential micro gestures hold in shaping a successful business trajectory. It invites readers to tune in to the silent language that often speaks louder than words, opening doors to a more profound understanding of the subtle dance of success in the business realm.

Chapter 2:

Effective Communication through Micro-gestures

In the heart of "Effective Communication through Micro-gestures," the exploration of the intricate dance of non-verbal communication dynamics takes centre stage. This chapter delves into the profound impact of micro-gestures on creating a bridge between individuals, transcending the limitations of spoken language.

Non-Verbal   Communication

Dynamics: The essence of this chapter lies in unravelling the intricate web of non-verbal cues that underpin human interaction. From subtle facial expressions to body language nuances, readers are guided through the subtleties that often communicate   more   than   words   alone. Understanding   the   dynamics   of   non-verbal communication becomes a gateway to enhancing the   richness   of   personal   and   professional connections.

As the chapter unfolds, readers gain insights into how   micro-gestures   contribute   to   the   overall effectiveness of communication.

The slight tilt of the head, the modulation of tone, or the pace of gestures—all become part of a silent dialogue that influences the way messages are received and interpreted. The narrative encourages readers to become adept observers, attuned to the unspoken language that shapes the dynamics of their interactions.

Moreover, the chapter underscores the role of micro-gestures in building rapport and establishing trust. By decoding non-verbal cues, individuals can foster a deeper connection with colleagues, clients, and partners.

Recognizing the significance of these subtle signals empowers readers to navigate communication challenges with finesse, whether in negotiations, presentations, or everyday conversations.

In essence, "Effective Communication through Micro-gestures" propels readers into a realm where the unsaid becomes as important as the said. It emphasises the mastery of non-verbal communication dynamics as an indispensable skill for anyone seeking to excel in personal and professional spheres.

This chapter lays the groundwork for readers to not only understand the silent language of micro gestures but also to harness its power for more impactful and nuanced communication.

NOTE

Effective non-verbal communication, encompassing skills in body language, eye contact, and gestures, is crucial for achieving success in business, particularly in financial negotiations where it fosters understanding and trust.

Chapter 3:

Leadership and Trust Building:

Leading with Subtle Influence and Micro gestures for Trust and Authority

Within the pages of "Leadership and Trust Building," the narrative unfolds into a dual exploration: leading with subtle influence and employing micro gestures to establish trust and authority.

This term unveils the artistry of leadership, demonstrating how the fusion of

nuanced influence and intentional non-verbal cues lays the foundation for trust within teams and organisations.

Leading with Subtle Influence: The chapter begins by unravelling the concept of leading with subtle influence, showcasing how effective leaders often wield influence with finesse rather than force. It explores the notion that true leadership extends beyond directives, emphasising the importance of inspiring and guiding through subtle cues. Leaders are encouraged to understand the impact of their influence on team dynamics, steering towards a leadership style that motivates and empowers rather than dictates.

Micro-gestures for Trust and Authority: The narrative seamlessly transitions into the realm of micro-gestures, highlighting their instrumental role in fostering trust and authority. Readers are guided through a spectrum of non-verbal cues, from maintaining open and approachable body language to active listening. Micro gestures become the silent architects of trust, conveying authenticity, empathy, and a genuine commitment to the well-being of the team.

As the exploration deepens, the chapter unveils the delicate balance between trust and authority.

Leaders are prompted to recognize how micro-gestures can project both approachability and decisiveness, creating a dynamic where trust is not compromised by authority. Subtle cues, such as acknowledging individual contributions or providing constructive feedback with empathy, emerge as powerful tools in establishing a leadership presence that commands respect and fosters a culture of trust.

Real-world examples and practical insights punctuate the chapter, illustrating how leaders who master the interplay of subtle influence and micro-gestures create environments where trust becomes the cornerstone of high-performance teams.

Through the lens of this chapter, leadership transforms into an art form, where the canvas is painted with the brushstrokes of authenticity, influence, and the silent language of micro-gestures. It stands as a guide for leaders seeking to navigate the intricate terrain of trust-building, wielding influence with grace and establishing authority through the power of subtle

cues.

Micro-gestures, like eye contact and

confident posture,

subtly build trust and authority,

influencing perceptions in

communication and fostering positive

impressions in social and professional

interactions.

Chapter 4:

Strategic Networking with Micro gestures:

Unlocking Networking Secrets and Adapting Micro-gestures Across Cultures

"Strategic Networking with Micro gestures" unfolds as a roadmap to navigate the intricate world of professional connections. This act, divided into two pivotal segments, delves into unlocking the secrets of networking and adapting micro gestures across diverse cultural landscapes.

Unlocking Networking Secrets: This

term initiates with the exploration of unlocking the secrets of networking through micro gestures. It unveils the understanding that successful networking extends beyond the exchange of business cards and polished introductions. Micro-gestures become the silent keys that open doors to meaningful connections. Readers are guided through the nuances of building rapport and establishing trust through subtle cues, such as a confident handshake, genuine eye contact, or a welcoming smile.

The narrative emphasises that mastering these micro-gestures transforms networking from a transactional exchange to a genuine connection that can pave the way for unforeseen opportunities.

Adapting Micro Gestures Across Cultures:

The narrative seamlessly transitions into the second segment, highlighting the critical importance of adapting micro gestures across diverse cultural contexts. The chapter navigates the delicate terrain of cross-cultural communication, underscoring that what may be considered a positive gesture in one culture could carry a different connotation in another.

Readers are equipped with practical insights into navigating the subtleties of micro-gestures, ensuring that their networking efforts are respectful, inclusive, and effective across the global business landscape.

As readers delve deeper into this chapter, they uncover the profound impact of culturally sensitive micro-gestures on forging connections that transcend geographical boundaries. Through real-world examples and pragmatic advice, the chapter serves as a guide for professionals seeking to elevate their networking skills.

It underscores the transformative power of micro-gestures in cultivating a global network that reflects cultural awareness, authenticity, and the finesse required to navigate the complexities of international business relationships.

NOTE

In global business, it's crucial to adapt micro-gestures for success. Respect diverse cultures; gestures like nods or handshakes may have different meanings. Mastering these subtleties helps in effective communication and financial negotiations.

Chapter 5

Financial Wisdom through Micro-gestures:

Small Financial Actions for Long-Term Prosperity and Smart Savings, Mindful Spending, and Wise Investing.

"Financial Wisdom through Micro-gestures" unfolds as a compass guiding readers through the intricate landscape of personal finance. This term, divided into two key segments, explores the transformative power of small financial actions and the strategic approach to smart savings, mindful spending, and wise investing.

Small Financial Actions for Long-Term Prosperity: The term financial wisdom begins by illuminating the significance of small financial actions as building blocks for long-term prosperity. Readers are ushered into the understanding that financial success is not solely about major decisions but is shaped by the cumulative impact of everyday choices. From setting aside a percentage of income for savings to making incremental increases in investment contributions, these micro-gestures emerge as the silent architects of enduring financial well-being.

The narrative encourages readers to cultivate a mindset of delayed gratification, where small sacrifices today pave the way for substantial financial growth tomorrow.

Smart Savings, Mindful Spending, and Wise Investing: Transitioning seamlessly into the second segment, the chapter delves into the strategic approach of smart savings, mindful spending, and wise investing. Readers are guided through the importance of intentional choices in savings, avoiding impulse spending, and making informed investment decisions.

The narrative unfolds practical strategies, such as creating an emergency fund, budgeting with purpose, and diversifying investment portfolios. Each micro gesture within this segment becomes a thread woven into the fabric of financial success, emphasising that thoughtful financial decisions, no matter how small, contribute significantly to the achievement of long-term prosperity.

It provides direction for those looking to... navigate the intricate world of personal finance, encouraging them to recognize the transformative power of small, intentional actions in shaping a secure and prosperous financial future.

Chapter 6:

Holistic Growth and Technology**

Holistic growth in the digital age is intricately tied to technology, incorporating personal development micro-gestures and navigating the digital landscape with technological finesse.

Personal Development Micro gestures:

These small, intentional actions play a pivotal role in fostering holistic well-being. Empowered by technology, individuals can leverage apps, trackers, and virtual communities to track progress, set meaningful goals, and cultivate self-awareness.

From mindfulness apps to fitness trackers, technology acts as an enabler for personal development micro gestures, encouraging a balanced and mindful lifestyle.

Navigating the Digital Landscape with Technological Micro-gestures: Utilise technology with apps, trackers, and virtual communities for holistic well-being. From mindfulness to fitness, it empowers personal development micro gestures, fostering balance and mindfulness in daily life.

Conclusion

In 'Micro-gestures for Macro Success,' the book delves into the transformative power of subtle actions in business and finance. It explores how seemingly inconsequential gestures lead to significant triumphs. By deciphering communication nuances, readers gain skills to navigate corporate success. The guide asserts that success lies in finer details, urging individuals to harness micro gestures for substantial gains in the dynamic tapestry of professional triumphs.

Embark on a journey
through Micro gestures
for Macro Success
by
[Williams L. Batts]
Uncover the secrete
Language
of success in the
tiny yet mighty gestures that
shape's our destinies